Wilbur Wings His Way Home

Written by
Wendy Morgan Burrell

Illustrated by
Barbara Torke

Copyright © 2019 by Wendy Morgan Burrell

All Rights Reserved.
No part of this book may be reproduced for any reason, by any means, including any method of photographic or digital reproduction, without the permission of the publisher, except by a reviewer who may quote brief passages in a review to be printed in a newspaper, magazine or journal. For permission requests, contact the publisher: https://www.sanjuanpub.com/contact-reprint-permission/

First Edition
Printed in the United States
10 9 8 7 6 5 4 3 2 1
ISBN: 978-1-7336234-2-1
BISAC: JUV002040 Juvenile Fiction / Animals / Birds

Book and cover design: Kathryn R. Burke
https://www.sanjuanpub.com/product/wilbur-wings-his-way-home/

San Juan Publishing Group, Inc.
P.O. Box 945, Montrose CO 81402
sanjuanpublishing.com

Dedicated to
Montrose Animal Protection Agency
of Montrose, Colorado
for all they do to stem the tide of pet overpopulation
and to educate young people about pet care.

Praise for Wilbur Wings His Way Home

"A delightful book that is sure to intrigue young readers. Practical information at the end of the story educates and encourages children to have an interest in the animal world. The illustrations are wonderful and add a beautiful element to the story through pictures."
~Sharon Penasa, Montrose Elementary School, After School Program Coordinator

One fine Saturday morning, Wilbur the Parakeet found himself being taken from the neighborhood pet shop, the only place he had ever known, to a home with a family of five. The dad, mom, and three young children were excited as could be to finally have their first pet ever.

In his new home, Wilbur was put into a very nice new birdcage on a stand. He had toys, a mirror for admiring himself, water and food cups, plus a fine perch upon which to sit.

The family was very attentive to Wilbur's needs. They covered him at night, and made certain that his cage was not in a cool or drafty spot. They talked to him on a regular basis as they went about their daily chores, and Wilbur responded with happy tweets.

Not long into his new life, the youngest of the three children started itching, sneezing, and wheezing. Wilbur heard words like, "must be allergic," and "too bad," and "can't keep." The oldest child even suggested rehoming the youngest child instead of Wilbur. "No way," said the parents.

The next thing Wilbur knew, a new family came to take him to their home. The mom, dad, and little red-headed boy carefully placed him in their living room within sight of a window. It overlooked a shady part of the lush green lawn, which was filled with an abundance of tall trees, blooming shrubs, and flowers.

The little red-headed boy loved Wilbur, talking to him, feeding him, and covering his cage at night, then greeting him in the mornings with bright, cheery words.

One day, when he was cleaning Wilbur's cage, the little red-headed boy let Wilbur out to fly about the living room to stretch his wings. Little did he realize that earlier the window by Wilbur's cage had been opened. Wilbur, upon discovering the window ajar, flew out and into the shady green yard that he had so often longed to visit.

Parakeets are not meant to be let outside on their own. After the first few hours of happy freedom, Wilbur was faced with the harsh reality of being outside.

He found himself to be hungry and thirsty, but when he was able to find some water to drink, a humongous cat approached him stealthily, licking his lips and chattering at him.

Soon it became dark and Wilbur longed for the safety and comforts of his cage. Other birds he spoke to were of no help at all. Not one of them responded to his chirps for help.

Wilbur huddled close to the trunk of a thick Colorado Spruce tree at night, hoping to be safe from a huge hawk he saw fly by at dusk.

During the day, Wilbur flew from tree to tree, bush to bush, and house to house, looking for that open window with his roomy, safe cage nearby.

Meantime, Wilbur's family was frantically searching and calling for him. They even placed his cage outside near the house leaving the door wide open for Wilbur in case he should find his way home.

One day, Wilbur heard voices calling his name, fading in and out with the wind through the trees.

He flew toward the voices and, bit by bit, the voices of his family were closer and then, there they were! The red-headed boy with his mom and dad were calling and looking for him! A delighted Wilbur flew to them as fast as his little wings could fly! He perched on the little boy's finger and trilled a very happy little song.

Wilbur was happy to be taken home, being held softly in the dad's big hands. Back in his cage, Wilbur sang a sweet song of homecoming. He was content to be in his comfortable cage with his toys and his mirror and his family nearby. Wilbur vowed to never more roam from home.

All About Parakeets

Parakeets, also known as Budgies, make wonderful pets, but as with any animal, there are some important facts to understand.

- Parakeets are active birds and need to exercise every day.
- Parakeets that live in small cages should be allowed out in a secure area for a couple of hours every day.
- Budgies need a diet of a variety of vegetables, leafy greens, and grains.
- Parakeets are about eight inches in length.
- Parakeets live between five and twelve years.
- Budgies love to play and explore.
- Purchase a cage that is longer than it is wide, so the Budgie can flit from perch to perch to get some exercise.
- Budgies can learn to whistle and talk.
- Parakeets come in many colors, most often blue, green, or yellow. They are dimorphic meaning male birds tend to be more colorful than the females.
- Male parakeets develop a bluish-purple ceres in maturity. Females have tan or brown ceres.
- Use of cleaning agents around the bird can be harmful.
- Household temperatures should not drop below 66 degrees, nor should they exceed 80 degrees.
- Don't place the cage in front of a heat or air conditioning vent.

Resources

https://pets.thenest.com

101 Facts About Parakeets by Julia Barnes

All About Your Budgerigar by Bradly Vinner

Amazing Facts and Pictures About Parakeets by Sandra Klaus

Parakeets: Everything About Purchase, Care, Nutrition Breeding, and Behavior by Annette Wolter

Parakeets (Let's Read About Pets) by JoAnn Early Macken

Pet Parakeets by Cecelia H. Brannon

Glossary

Ajar - open

Budgie - another name for parakeet

Ceres - the waxy-fleshy covering at the base of the upper beak

Chattering - the chirping noise a cat sometimes makes when watching birds or other prey.

Dimorphic - the sex of the bird can be determined by its coloration.

Humongous - very large

Rehoming - being placed in a different home

Secure - free from danger

Stealthily - very quietly, sneaking up on

About the Author

Wendy Burrell, a retired teacher, has worked in the humane education field most of her adult life, teaching after school and summer classes about animals and pet care. During Be Kind to Animals Week (the first full week in May), Wendy teams with Montrose Animal Shelter staff members to teach safety around animals as well as proper pet care to area elementary students. *Wilbur Wings His Way Home* came to be when Wendy couldn't locate a picture book about bird care to share with her students.

About the Illustrator

Barbara Torke has been painting since she was a child growing up on Colorado's Front Range. In college, she studied art and education, earning her BA and MA degrees. She taught at the elementary level as well as several other subjects and grades. Barbara is best known for her whimsical watercolors and pastels, many of dogs and pickup trucks. She has illustrated several children's books. *Wilbur Wings His Way Home* combines three of her great loves: painting, storytelling, and books.